M000283687

MEDIA: FROM CHAOS TO CLARITY

FIVE GLOBAL TRUTHS THAT MAKE SENSE OF A MESSY MEDIA WORLD

By Judy Ungar Franks

MEDIA: FROM CHAOS TO CLARITY

FIVE GLOBAL TRUTHS THAT MAKE SENSE OF A MESSY MEDIA WORLD

By Judy Ungar Franks

The Marketing Democracy, Ltd.
2011, USA, Chicago

Media: From Chaos to Clarity
Five Global Truths That Make Sense of a Messy Media World
By Judy Ungar Franks
Copyright © 2011 by The Marketing Democracy, Ltd.

All rights reserved. No part of this book may be reproduced by any means in any form, photocopied, recorded, electronic or otherwise, without the written permission from the publisher except for brief quotations in a review.

ISBN: 978-0-9834662-1-5

Printed in the United States of America by Quartet Digital Printing, Evanston, Illinois.
10 9 8 7 6 5 4 3 2 1

Published by The Marketing Democracy, Ltd.

the
marketing
Democracy

Web site: www.themarketingdemocracy.com

Disclaimer: This book provides general information that is intended to inform and educate the reader on a general basis. Every effort has been made to assure that the information contained herein is accurate and timely as of the date of this publication. However, it is provided for the convenience of the reader only. Reliance on the information in this book is at the reader's sole risk. In no event, are the Author, Publisher or any affiliated party liable for any direct, indirect, incidental, consequential or other damages of any kind whatsoever including lost profits, relative to the information or advice provided herein. Reference to any specific product, process or service, does not constitute an endorsement or recommendation.

For James

Thank you for showing me that there is clarity from chaos if you are willing look at the world in entirely new ways.

TABLE OF CONTENTS

FOREWORD

I grew up in a world of linear media. My mother saved every copy of the LIFE and National Geographic magazines she ever received. Everyone in town read the local newspaper. Late night radio station XELO in Juarez sold live baby chickens, shipped directly to your home (going cheap, cheap, cheap). And my father, a true new product buff, bought one of the first TV sets in our town. Neighbors would come and sit in our living room for hours, just watching the test patterns and remarking on what a marvel that was.

When I finally went to work, the first job I had was with a trade publication. I then made my way to a daily newspaper. As an advertising agency account executive, I bartered the sides of milk cartons for TV and radio airtime for my dairy client.

So I have been in or around media all my life.

And, over the past half-dozen years, I must confess that, being a digital media immigrant, I have had some difficulty keeping up with all the new innovations. That's not to mean I am a true Luddite, only a partial one. (After all, I do own an Osborne 1, the first non-portable, portable computer.)

Media today is complex, difficult, confusing and, most of all, irrational to a person who grew up with "Mr. Rogers Neighborhood" and "American Bandstand." That was a world where the media sent out programming at their convenience and the family gathered around to watch the TV or, if you're as old as I am, to "watch the radio" ... Jack Benny, Fred Allen, the afternoon adventure serials like Jack Armstrong and others.

When Judy Franks first came to me with the manuscript for this book, "Media: From Chaos to Clarity," it was like all my dreams had come true. Here, in my hands, was a short, succinct text that put today's media world in perspective. A concept and approach that finally explained why and how and in what ways media was changing ... and what it meant to all of us going forward.

I have been trying to make sense of all the changes in the media for both students and practitioners for more years than I like to count. This is the first book, tome, discussion or whatever you want to call it that really makes some sense of what is going on in the media world today.

Judy is a professional media person. One of the few who can really "think" about media, not just push the buttons and read the slides to clients. She has a unique knack of making the difficult seem obvious, the challenging seem easy and the complex sound simple. In short, she has a truly unique view of the media world ... one that she is sharing in this text.

To me, Judy has done something remarkable in this book. She has explained the changes in media and communications in terms we've never used before. She understands networks and systems and circles and synergy and interactions, where most media and marketing communications people still think in lines and arrows and outputs. Judy deals with the present and the future. And that's what's important.

We'll never put the digital media genie back in the bottle no matter how much we try. We'll never recapture the old days of "appointment television." We'll never go back to 5-pound cell phones that can't get a signal. We are in a totally new media world.

Fortunately, we have Judy Franks to explain that new world to and for us. Yes, there is media chaos all around us. But Judy understands the chaos and can help all of us find our own way through it, whether we're a marketer, an agency, a media owner or even a Luddite-like professor.

Read on. Learn. Enjoy. But, most of all, begin to understand the new world of media that surround all of us. It's the world we live in today. And while it will likely change tomorrow, we can begin to understand where we are going with the "Five Global Truths" as our compass.

Let Judy lead you there as she has done with me.

Don Schultz
Professor
Integrated Marketing Communications Department
Medill, Northwestern University

PREFACE

If we are going to spend some quality time together through the pages of this book, I owe you an introduction! An author should not just show up uninvited. Sure, you may have picked up this book because you either work in or are interested in the topic of media. Perhaps you heard the text was "a good read" that offers an insightful view of the media world today. Maybe, the book was assigned to you as required reading, and you really had no choice! Regardless of your reason for opening the book, you need to be assured that our conversation will be time well-spent, and that this text will offer you insights into the messy media world that surrounds us.

My name is Judy Franks, and I am a faculty member in the Integrated Marketing Communications Department of Medill, Northwestern University. I developed and now teach an undergraduate course in the IMC certificate program: IMC 304 Media and Message Delivery. My point of view, both in the classroom and in this book, is shaped by both theory and practice.

Prior to joining the faculty of Medill, I spent 23 years as a practitioner in the agency world. I rose to the executive leadership ranks of Chicago's leading advertising and media services agencies: Leo Burnett, Euro RSCG Chicago (formerly known as TLK), Starcom and Energy BBDO. This experience gave me a hands-on perspective on how the media work and how the application of several academic theories of media effects could actually connect customers with brands in the marketplace.

During the past quarter century, the media world changed exponentially. I experienced these changes firsthand, across a myriad of client situations, customer targets and global markets. In every case, the media plans radically changed from an emphasis on television, with a smattering of other media for good measure, to a sophisticated combination of video, audio, text and social messages that traversed every screen imaginable!

All the while, the industry cobbled together strategies to plan for and measure outcomes in a media landscape that was changing around us in real time! We still relied on the established theories of media effects that were left over from a pre-digital media world, and we then augmented those theories with learning from market-mix models and real-time customer behavior. In essence, we created what I will call "coping mechanisms" for navigating uncharted waters.

When I set out to find a contemporary media text for my course, I could not find a text that described the media mess that we are currently dealing with in the real world. Many textbooks still talk about the media world as it was 25 years ago. They falsely assume that the thinking and the models that applied to a non-digital media world still make sense today. Sure, they cover "new/emerging" outlets such as digital, social and mobile media. But they do so as if these media are simply additional choices to consider when building a media plan. Where is the paradigm shift that marketers, media planners and the media are dealing with today?

If I couldn't find an accurate, contemporary view of the media world in textbooks, perhaps I would find what I was looking for in the business press instead. While I found bits and pieces in several places (see recommended reading list), I still came up short. Nowhere could I find a comprehensive explanation for the way the media world looks and operates today. Perhaps the idea of talking about the current state of the media is too daunting. In fact, it's chaos!

We live and work in an era that demands real-time accountability. The old media models reflect how it used to be. We have no choice but to create a new, common understanding of how the media work today. Not necessarily a deep dive on the inner workings of each medium, per se, but rather a new understanding of how media work together and how consumers shape their experiences across media to engage with content.

Where can we find a new point of view? It's sitting beneath the surface of what I call "media chaos," and it's waiting for us to discover and act upon it. You will soon read about "Five Global Truths" that make sense out of a messy media world. I cannot take credit for inventing these truths; I am simply reporting what already exists.

The Five Global Truths are an interpretation of how new technologies are creating new opportunities for those pioneers who are brave enough to try something new. What happens when you have the permission to strip away the media bias of a past era? All of a sudden, you can view the media world with a new clarity that makes a lot of sense.

I look forward to sharing this thinking with you in the coming chapters of the book. You may not agree with every point. Nor will every indicated action/next step be relevant to you. But I hope you will be inspired to look at the messy media world in a whole new light. And I hope that that the Five Global Truths will, in some way, help you to thrive in your pursuits.

Best Wishes,

Judy Ungar Franks

CHAPTER ONE

ONCE UPON A TIME

Once upon a time and not too long ago, the media, for all its variety, used to be fairly predictable. Newspapers delivered the daily news on our doorsteps. Magazines fueled our passions. Television was "must-see." Radio dominated drive time. And computers put a world of information at our fingertips. With reasonable accuracy, we could understand media audiences and the relative return on investments for using the various media to connect customers with brands.

Now, virtually all of those dependable, measurable media models are undergoing revolutionary change. Welcome to media chaos. We are living in what may be the most exciting and transformative time in the history of the media, and it's messy. What was once an orderly media system with predictable audiences and dependable business models has turned into a cross-platform firestorm that is exploding and imploding all at once. It's chaos! Literally.

Unfortunately, human beings aren't hardwired to deal with chaos. We like to know what to expect. We crave a sense of order. But, despite our desire for order, we deal with chaos in all aspects of our lives every day. When we walk out the door, we enter a chaotic world, and we don't give it much thought.

Perhaps we have developed coping mechanisms, a series of truisms that create some sense of order and purpose in our world despite the mess that surrounds us. These beliefs (aka Global Truths) enable us to navigate through and even thrive in chaos.

That's what this book is about. It's about new ways to talk and think about the media world in chaos. We need to think about the media world during this state of unprecedented transition and deal with it in brand new ways. If we're going to do the job that marketers still need, we need to teach ourselves and others about what's actually going on. Not what used to happen in a more orderly media world, but what is happening right now. If we intend to thrive during a period of extreme uncertainty and transformational change, we need to find and agree on the truisms that can help us to navigate media chaos.

It's a top-to-bottom job. And bottom to top. Students still need to learn how to become effective marketers, and marketers still need to build brands and drive commerce in a messy media world. And we all need to figure out how to talk to each other. Unfortunately, it's all easier said than done because we're all working with old software—understandings left over from how it used to be. We're still using thinking systems both in our classrooms and out in the workplace that do not adequately account for the new reality of the media. We still have books on our shelves that quantify—quite accurately—the way it used to be, yet have little relevance to how it is. The old rules simply don't fit, and many of the current conversations are far from productive.

We need to strike the following theories from our collective consciousness in order to move forward. Nothing good ever comes from doom and gloom. The past is not always a window to the future. And the technology, for all its glitz and glory, isn't the full story.

The Apocalypse Theory

(or the Sky Is Falling)

It's time to set the record straight. It isn't all doom and gloom, despite what the naysayers are saying (and, by the way, they make money by creating drama). Nothing is dying that doesn't deserve to die off on its own. We are confusing the death of old business models with the death of traditional media themselves. If you've been making easy money on business models that have fallen apart and you're not prepared to change, maybe it is doom and gloom. But the notion that new media is killing old media is simply untrue. Nothing dies unless it's weak to begin with. If a weak organism catches a virus, it dies. If a healthy organism catches a virus, it fights it off and actually becomes stronger.

What Is Past Is Prologue Theory

(or Apply Old Methods to New Media)

We can never truly move forward without an understanding of our past. But understanding the past and remaining stuck in the past are two very different things. The old rules of media that were based upon fixed distribution platforms, predictive audience aggregation and response functions simply cannot cope with the dynamics and complexity of the chaos. In fact, we are experiencing our version of quantum media that requires quantum media thinking. The old, Newtonian rules simply do not apply.

Carpe Technology Diem

(or Technology Rules Everything)

Every day, a new technology springs up that becomes the darling of the industry and the focus of our attention. We're focusing on the wrong thing! Technology is transient: Wait 10 minutes and it will change. The transient state of technology is no surprise: Moore's Law mandates it. If we build marketing practices around technology, we need to be prepared for those practices to have a short shelf life.

Where can we find answers? The answers are sitting right beneath the surface of chaos. We are starting to see patterns emerge that help to explain the media mess. They are presented in this book as the Five Global Truths.

We didn't simply "land" on the Five Global Truths that make sense out of a messy media world. Each one only became apparent after we sought out meaning from the new function of the media themselves. Some technological occurrence had to both illuminate and enable our explanation.

But, don't believe me. I'm just the author. For each of the Five Global Truths, there's evidence:

- *The Technology*: Something changes in the media itself.
- *The Pioneer*: Someone had an "aha" moment.
- *The Chaos*: All that's wrong with our approach today.
- *The Truth*: Somehow, it all makes sense.

If we can harness the learning from the Five Global Truths, we will be poised to flourish in media chaos and actually learn to enjoy it!

CHAPTER TWO

THE ERA OF EXPONENTIAL EFFECTS

Just one short generation ago, we lived and marketed in the Newtonian Media Era. The media systems were relatively stable, and the laws of marketing were absolute. Think about it. Our choices were limited to four major "above the line" media: television, radio, print and out of home. Each medium drew mass audiences in relatively predictable patterns, and we knew how to combine both inter-media and intra-media options to reach audiences and accumulate advertising effects. Even the most coveted medium of all, word of mouth, was simply a matter of engaging in and inspiring a one-on-one conversation.

In the Newtonian Media Era, we planned media allocations with authority and we presented outcomes based upon what were, at the time, irrefutable laws of media dynamics.

- **The Law of Recency (Erwin Ephron):**
  Advertising continuity and weekly reach are the best media scheduling practices to intercept a shopper as close to the purchase occasion as possible.
- **The Law of AdStock (Simon Broadbent):**
  Advertising accumulates effects over time (i.e., builds AdStock) and up to a point when it will begin to decay (half-life) without further support.

- **The Law of Effective Reach (Herb Krugman):**
  Consumers are more likely to respond after three
  exposures to a commercial message.

Although the laws actually conflicted with each other, it
didn't matter. Marketers could subscribe to a particular theory of
how advertising worked, and media planners could build a media
plan that would emulate the theory in the real world. Things
didn't change all that much from the media plan "on paper" to
the media plan "in market." We were able to model post-term
effects with relative statistical certainty.

During the late 20th century, things began to change. We
began to see a breakdown in the certainty of both the legacy
systems (the media themselves) and the legacy thinking (those
irrefutable laws). The world became less predictive, and our
actions yielded more relative outcomes in the marketplace. The
early signs of chaos began to emerge. Let's call this period the
Era of Media Relativity.

Why was the media world becoming less certain?
Actually, the biggest media transformation of modern times,
digital media, is not yet part of the story. While digital marketing
and its early manifestations as search and performance marketing
began to take hold toward the end of the 20th century, it really
didn't play much of a role in the transformation taking place
during the Era of Media Relativity. Rather, the true
transformation was caused by the legacy media themselves.

During the late 20thcentury, media capacity expanded
beyond our wildest imaginations. The legacy media went
through a radical transformation as the number of options
expanded. And the transformation was not a straight-line
trajectory of what we already knew and accepted as true. The
changes we were seeing in the media were somewhat of a

paradox and downright challenging to the conventions of our Newtonian media minds.

As capacity began to expand and more options became available, the media began to take on the properties of both mass and niche at the same time. This phenomenon occurred in practically every legacy medium: television, magazines, radio and newspapers. For example, television could now deliver mass audiences to prime-time "event" shows, while also catering to the niche tastes of a gardener, a cook or a fisherman through specialty cable networks. Magazines in the mass/general interest and women's service categories still enjoyed huge circulation figures while vertical special interest publications could also thrive by selling just a few hundred thousand copies. An AM news/talk radio station could still reach the majority of the local market during drive time while a jazz station could cater to the tastes of a select audience and hold its own on the FM band. And so on.

According to Newtonian media thinking, mass and niche should be diametrically opposed. In the classical calculations of reach and frequency, these two factors are mathematics trade-offs. How could the media take on both properties at once? This paradox simply didn't fit the commonly accepted understanding of how the media work.

The rapid expansion of media choices also made it increasingly difficult to predict audiences to particular media offerings with absolute certainty. Audiences became much more dynamic and difficult to pin down both within and across media. While, historically, we could count audience exposures with a fair degree of certainty, we now had to settle for probabilities and "opportunities to see" (OTS).

To make matters worse, that niche medium called "digital" had a completely different set of audience measurement rules associated with search and performance that made no sense in a world that was dominated by the laws of reach and frequency. Ironically, the new digital media could be measured in more absolute terms while the established legacy media became more relative in their performance.

Would the Era of Media Relativity create a new operating system and displace all of our Newtonian media laws? We needed our version of Heisenberg's Uncertainty Principle and the idea that "it all depends upon your perspective/your point of view."

Perhaps the birth of Context Planning was our answer to the relative state of the media. Now, in addition to counting, we looked for context. This idea made media selection more open for interpretation and judgment from the marketer, the account/media planner and the consumer. Could we expect the brand to show up in this particular context? Would the media placement fit? It depends. Surprisingly, Context Planning did not displace the Newtonian governance. In our industry's desire to hang on to fundamental truths, we continued to use these old rules and applied them to a media world that simply didn't behave the way it used to.

Thank goodness, it really doesn't matter anymore! The Era of Media Relativity is over. Welcome to the Era of Exponential Effects! The media landscape is changing around us in real time and in such profound ways that the entire experience can only be described as exponential.

Everything we knew to be true is now in question. Our media systems are in chaos, and they seem to be propelled by completely new laws of energy that have a truly exponential effect on marketing outcomes.

The New Law of Energy: C^3

The Era of Exponential Effects is fueled by the three Cs: consumers, content and channels. There is nothing new about the three primary ingredients in this equation. What has changed profoundly is the relationship of the three Cs to each other and the amplification of the effects.

1. *Consumers* have evolved from recipients of marketing to accelerants of marketing.

2. *Content* is no longer the stuff that fills stable media systems; rather, it is the magnet that attracts audiences and involves them in the marketing process.

3. *Channels* are now the ultimate wild card in the marketing plan. Channels are no longer controlled distribution systems for marketing messages, but rather the mechanism by which consumers can see, shape, share or reject marketing messages. Welcome to chaos!

C (1): Consumers

In the Era of Exponential Effects, consumers are no longer recipients; they are now accelerants. They used to be the end point; now they are a powerful intermediary. This is a much bigger idea than "consumer as media." Today's consumers can amplify marketing messages by exponential measures—by the size of their networks and at the speed of their connections.

This phenomenon creates a new reach potential of media and messaging activities beyond anyone's wildest dreams! How many consumers can we reach in the Era of Exponential Effects? The answer: We truly don't know! Reach takes on a whole new meaning. We can only measure the first step in a multi-step process where consumers quickly take over and control the true exposure potential of a brand's media plan.

Reach still begins as a measure of the opportunity to see a brand's message that was placed in a particular medium. However, what used to be the end point of the calculation is now just the first step in an exponential experience. A certain percentage of the audiences will actually see/hear/experience the message, and a portion of them will become truly engaged. An engaged consumer now has the ability to perpetuate and accelerate the message among his or her personal networks and across a myriad of media platforms.

Each individual network becomes a whole new audience to the marketing message—one that was not planned for or controlled by the marketer (or the media for that matter). The consumer now acts as a media channel with its own built-in audience (friends, fans, followers, e-mail lists etc.). And the cycle continues.

What is the true reach of a media plan? It depends on two key factors: (1) How many people did you engage in the first place? and (2) How far and wide did the message travel among each engaged consumer's network? The answer to both questions is: "We really don't know!"

There is also a downside to this consumer dynamic: Consumers now have the ability to accelerate the demise of media effects. Consumers always had the power to avoid and ignore commercial messages in any medium. Now it's just more transparent to the marketer. Consumer avoidance isn't the full story. For instance, imagine if you anger a consumer. What happens when consumers can register their disdain across network platforms that have exponential reach potential? You are left with contra-marketing initiatives that can overpower the brand's own voice.

C (2): Content

The role of content and the role of channel are often confused. It's time to set the record straight. Media cannot attract audiences; only content has the power to attract and engage an audience. Content is the glue that holds everything together. Without great content, media are transient and perishable. The channels themselves no longer have the capability to attract and sustain an audience. The media are nothing more than transient pipeline.

Once upon a time, the media could build audiences on their own. Not anymore. The ability of any medium to create an audience dissipated as soon as consumers were faced with an abundance of choice. Once the media began to expand beyond a few limited options, consumers had the choice to opt in to specific content offerings that suited their interests. The content that was served in a particular channel became the audience magnet rather than the channel itself.

Dr Mark Maiville presented this finding to the ARF Audience Measurement Symposium back in 2007. His work, titled "A Thin Sliced World: New Methods, Models and Systems for Media Audience Analysis," demonstrated that media audiences are nothing more than millions of individual consumers exercising their content preferences on their available channels. Consumers find content that is relevant to them, and they ignore the rest.

Great content can traverse the boundaries of any particular media platform to become what we now call a transmedia experience. In his 2006 book "Convergence Culture," Henry Jenkins describes a world where content creators can tell stories across media platforms and "in ways that each medium makes distinctive contributions to our collective understanding."

27

An engaged fan is more than willing to traverse channels to deepen his or her experience with the transmedia story.

While the entertainment industry is quickly adopting a transmedia content model, the marketing industry has been slow to follow. Marketers still craft individual channel strategies and then develop content to suit the channel. Transmedia marketing campaigns are few and far between. In the new energy equation, marketers must shift their focus toward the creation of compelling content that is suited for a transmedia experience.

C (3): Channels

Channels have become the real wild card in the equation. What was once a relatively fixed distribution system for the dissemination of content has now become incredibly amorphous and downright chaotic. What happened? Welcome to the digital media revolution.

In the first decade of the 21st century, digital was no longer something tied to a computer screen; rather, nearly every media platform known to man became digital in some form. This digital transformation destabilized the entire media ecosystem. The digitized nature of the media enabled consumers to displace content from one channel and send it along another digital pathway without much, if any, intervention from the content producer. Content can now fall right through the cracks or travel beyond our wildest imaginations.

If media channels are now unstable and content can jump off one medium and onto another, what is the value of a media plan? Is this another case of marketers trying to hang onto the past and cling to the notion that they still have control over the brand experience? Has the media plan become nothing more than an expensive piece of paper that yields a false sense of security?

Marketers desperately want to keep media channels in their historical perspective and treat them as fixed distribution systems. Those days are indeed gone. But a loss of control doesn't mean that we should walk away from a blueprint. We simply have to acknowledge two fundamental changes to the contemporary media plan. First, the architectural process is now shared between the professional and the consumer. Second, media pathways cannot be fully charted until the journey is complete.

Thank goodness consumers are now co-creators in the marketing of brands. Frankly, they are having a much easier time living in media chaos. They don't ask why; they simply consume unfathomable amounts of all types of media and shape their experiences as they go. We are stuck with the why. Integrated Marketing Communications (IMC) cannot deteriorate into chaos simply because we can't wrap our heads around the exponential changes in the media universe. It's time to make sense of the messy media world. It's time to uncover the Global Truths.

CHAPTER THREE

THE FIVE GLOBAL TRUTHS

How can we harness the new power and potential of C^3 – channels, content and consumers? It's easier said than done! When one of the three key elements–channels–is in a state of total flux, and the other two are exhibiting their own dynamics, we're looking at a challenge of some size.

Perhaps if we look beyond all the disruptions and distractions, we might be able to see patterns and purpose. Maybe media chaos isn't so complex after all. Einstein said it best, "If you can't explain it simply, you don't understand it well enough." Is it possible that there are simple explanations for the seismic shifts in the media universe?

Oftentimes, there are simple explanations buried beneath all the problems. You simply have to get to the root of the problem! As a first step, let's get the problems out on the table. When you listen to all the complaints that run rampant in the press, in the conference rooms of Fortune 500 companies and their agencies and among the media themselves, you can begin to classify them into five macro themes.

Each of the five problems listed here reveals a core truth that helps us understand this new media world we're living in. Quite often they're a path to new opportunity. And they're definitely about new ways of looking at the world of media.

Problem #1: Media Identity Crisis

Media channels used to be separate and distinct from one another. Each medium had a specific function/utility in our lives. We used to talk on phones, watch video content on televisions and surf for information on computers. Now? The media are tripping over each other! We can do practically all of the above on any screen device. How can we tell the media apart? How do we know when to use specific media and for what purpose/function? What content belongs on what medium?

Global Truth #1: Convergence

Let's take another look at the media identity crisis. Perhaps the orientation of the media has shifted. What used to be separate and distinct is now a coming together of platforms. The media can now be explained with one word: convergence. With digitization, media are becoming strikingly similar. Not the same, exactly, but really quite similar when you think about it. And most of them are interconnecting and converging through some sort of digital interface. Each new media vehicle and delivery mechanism serves to blur the lines further. What was once separate is now the same. And, more often than not, it will come with a screen!

Nielsen calls this the "three screen phenomenon." But the three screens are just the beginning.

Problem # 2: Winners and Losers

There is so much "new media" to contend with every day, how can we predict the winners and the losers? When figuring out how to handle a media budget, this is no small question. Which media deserves our attention and investment?

Which media should sustain the inevitable marketing budget cut? Which media will be around in the next five years, three years or even one year? There are some questions that we need to keep asking – particularly since the media landscape keeps on changing. We want to invest in the winners and not spend our budgets with the losers. That's true for venture capitalists, marketers and the media themselves.

Global Truth #2: Symbiosis

Perhaps there are no clear winners and losers anymore. The emerging media will align themselves with the existing media to create mutually beneficial, working relationships. The age-old notion of survival of the fittest is giving way to a more cooperative and collaborative system in nature: symbiosis. The media operate in a symbiotic relationship. The media do not kill each other; they reinforce each other!

Just look at the relationship between television and YouTube. In theory, YouTube should have become a major threat to television as consumers could now "broadcast themselves." In reality, television and YouTube support and reinforce each other. Both are stronger because they co-exist.

Disappointed? There's more drama in "winners and losers," but the fact remains: The media collaborate despite our best efforts to pit one against the other. While it's true that individual media vehicles may come and go, that's "creative destruction at work." But don't confuse evolution with extinction.

Working with this new global truth will be based on understanding how the new media life forms are operating. There will be (and already are) exciting new combinations that will deliver powerful experiences.

Problem #3: Faulty Wiring

Content doesn't seem to stay put anymore. It seems to go wherever consumers want it to go. We can try to control it, but it seems to leak, short-circuit and show up on different pathways. Not only that, but content rarely travels untouched across a distribution pathway without something happening to it. Content either vaporizes or it lands on alternate distribution pathways or it attracts additional comment–for better or worse. That being the case, how can we build media plans with any confidence that the content we place on any particular channel will travel from Point A to Point B with limited disruption? Previously, this was never a problem. Now it is.

Global Truth #3: Circuits

Perhaps the media aren't "faulty" at all. Programmers and marketers no longer control the media circuits; consumers do. We already understand consumer control as "pull marketing." But what we are seeing is far more profound than pull. Rather, consumers can displace content from any media channel and either: (1) vaporize it because it isn't any good or (2) share great content across other channels/networks.

We used to believe that each medium functioned as a closed circuit that ran in parallel to other media. Thanks to convergence, the circuits are now open and content can flow freely across platforms. Ask Viacom, and they will tell you how their copyrighted content first landed on YouTube. They didn't put it there!

Problem #4: Living Beyond Purpose

Have the media outlived their function/utility? Once upon a time, we needed towers to broadcast signals to a designated market area (DMA). We needed elaborate

34

distribution networks to access news and entertainment on the printed page. Our choices were bound by the bandwidth of the spectrum and the cost of paper, ink and postage. Specific media used to be a necessary distribution pathway to reach specific audiences. To some extent, they had audience exclusivity. Today, thanks to technology enhancements, it seems that no single medium has an "exclusive" on either its method of distribution or the audience it serves. The media have become redundant. More important, what is the new role for the media in this redundant media ecosystem?

Global Truth #4: Brands

While it may be true that many media have outlived their functional utility, perhaps the media can take on a whole new purpose if we reframe them not as products but as brands. The brand concept is no longer about a product or service. It's about pretty much everything. It's time to bring a healthy dose of brand management to the business of the media.

Media have the potential to become cross-platform destinations for an engaging content experience that is grounded in a promise between the brand and the customer. Thanks to its emphasis on brand management, ESPN doesn't have to worry about the ever-changing media landscape. Its brand experience can easily migrate across any media platform, present and future.

More and more, successful media channels are behaving as brands. Meanwhile, many successful brands are behaving like media. Just take a look at Nike and Starbucks and you will get a glimpse of the future today. These brands do not necessarily need to rely upon other media to deliver their message to consumers. They have their own distribution networks to deliver engaging, high quality content experiences directly to their customer base.

Problem #5: Who Pays the Bills?

Does anyone know how to make money anymore? Hundred year-old business models are falling apart. Fragmenting audiences are just one of the financial problems plaguing the media. Not being able to charge for content is another. We started giving stuff away for free, either because we thought it didn't matter or we had to when we discovered that no one would pay for it. Now audiences are migrating to the "free stuff" and we can't figure out how to charge them back. What's the new financial formula for success?

Global Truth #5: Economics

Perhaps the laws of supply and demand haven't changed at all. Maybe we just forgot about them as we built faulty business models. The search for sustainable business models will be a particular challenge for media that have been operating on older business models that haven't kept up with changes or consumer preferences. This will be a moving target for quite some time, but here's one thing we can all count on: Consumers will pay for quality content that is in limited supply and in high demand.

Think about the whole concept of premium cable. For years, consumers were willing to pay an additional fee to access content that was truly superior to the basic offering. Consumers didn't pay for HBO because they wanted or needed another cable channel. Rather, consumers assigned real value to HBO's brand of pre-eminent storytelling. The unique content experience justified the premium price for this network.

At the same time, consumers are less inclined to pay for distribution that is transient and redundant. That's why the cable companies are in a price war with satellite providers and ISPs and mobile network carriers are trying to lock up consumers in multi-year contracts. Consumers can now shop for access at the lowest price!

Economics is the final challenge: arriving at a business model that delivers value to marketers and allows media management to make an honest profit. Media profits fuel investments in content. And high quality content is the glue that holds this messy media system together.

Now What?

We now have a framework; the Five Global Truths that help explain a messy media world:

- **Truth #1: Convergence**
- **Truth #2: Symbiosis**
- **Truth #3: Circuits**
- **Truth #4: Brands**
- **Truth #5: Economics**

In the coming chapters, we will explore each truth individually and in detail. We will then identify how these themes all come together to create a stunning big picture.

There is an exciting media world waiting for both students and professionals who can embrace and act upon these new truths. In the coming chapters, we will see how leveraging these new ways of looking at the media can generate new energy and success. We will meet some of the pioneers—those already acting upon these truths. And, in the very near future, one of those successful pioneers, the visionaries making it happen in this new world of media, might very well be you!

CHAPTER FOUR

GLOBAL TRUTH #1 CONVERGENCE

Convergence: n. the merging of distinct technologies, industries or devices into a unified whole.

(Source: Merriam-webster.com).

A Buzzword That's Truly Buzz-Worthy!

Convergence is a hot buzzword, and deservedly so! What can this book possibly illuminate about the topic of convergence that you, the reader, don't already know? And why is this phenomenon the first "Global Truth" that can explain media chaos?

The answer is quite simple: We used to operate in a world where the media were separate and distinct. We built an entire industry, along with business models and marketing practices, that treated each medium as its own entity. We created the irrefutable laws of media dynamics that factored effects one medium at a time.

Now the media are coming together. The old models simply don't fit a convergence paradigm. Our thinking and our practices need to catch up. We need to come together to find holistic solutions.

Different Media for Different Times

To readers who don't distinguish much between their television, their computer, their tablet or their smart phone, this entire chapter may seem completely "old school" and out of touch. But we have to deal with the unfortunate reality that our existing systems and thinking are left over from a time when the media world was actually quite different. Media convergence simply didn't exist. The media fundamentally worked in very different ways.

During the Newtonian Media Era, and even during the Era of Media Relativity, the media used to be different from one another. The technology platforms were different. The content was different. We used different media to serve different needs. We "talked" on telephones. We "listened" to the radio. We "read" printed pages of newspapers and magazines. And we used the computer as a "lean forward" device to seek out a universe of information that lived on the Web. Stop and think about how different things were not too long ago: The only personal medium that served up video content was your television!

In this world, each medium accumulated effects in its own unique way. Some media were known for building audience reach while others were good at adding message frequency to the media plan. And we could plan various combinations of the media (i.e., the media mix) based upon the idea of media quintiles: Some consumers tended to be heavy users of a particular medium and a light user of others. By combining media and creating a mix, we could manipulate the levels of target audience reach and frequency in order to deliver the desired outcome.

That was then, and this is now. Media convergence is manifesting in an important way. Frankly, every medium now comes along with a "screen." Why is this happening now?

The Technology That Changed Everything

Digital technology changed the face of media in profound ways. Every medium imaginable now has some form of a digital structure to it. Digital used to be reserved for computers. Now every medium is either completely digital or has a digital offering. That means the basic technology structure of the media is now more similar than dissimilar. How did this structure manifest? Nearly every medium today has a screen interface. Think about it. Until recently, only three types of screens enjoyed critical mass: movie screens, television screens and computer screens. Now? Every media platform imaginable can offer a screen interface: phones, mp3 players, outdoor billboards, newspapers, magazines, books. You name it!

The screen phenomenon became so prolific that the behemoth television research company A.C. Nielsen began to publish a "Three Screen" Report. Although the report only covers three screens (TV, computer and mobile phone screens), at least it's a step in the right direction! The report quantifies our intuition and what, frankly, the younger media generation already accepts as true: Consumers of all ages are consuming more video across more screens than ever before. The new common denominator is video. And video can show up on any screen.

Technology Changes All the Rules

If digital technology gave every medium imaginable a screen that can carry video content, how will this affect the old-world laws of media effects? Will media still accumulate effects the same way? The laws are still taught in our classrooms and practiced out in the marketplace. But they don't seem to work quite the way they used to. We are now experiencing our own version of warp physics. Some basic truths that we thought were true are now true in reverse!

1. Reach is now frequency. What used to be "reach" is now "frequency." Not so long ago, we needed to use a combination of multiple media formats (i.e., multi-media mix) to reach a broad consumer demographic with our marketing messages. Why? Because we used to see a significant divide in media consumption between the digital media natives and the rest of us. Media quintile data illustrated clear patterns of media preference: Certain demographic cohorts were heavy users of one medium and light to non-users of others. The media mix was, therefore, crucial to add reach, to ensure that "everyone" saw the brand's message.

Not anymore. We have mounting evidence that consumers are consuming vast amounts of all media. There are no longer trade-offs: Consumers simply add a new screen to their repertoire and keep all the rest. We're just spending more time interacting with more screens! This has a profound impact on the role of media mix: All of a sudden, a multi-media mix is driving frequency along with reach.

This reversal of media effects—reach is now frequency—has profound implications for how we think about and schedule video communications. If the same piece of video communication—let's say a television commercial or some variant of the commercial—appears on both the television screen and the computer screen, we can expect the video to wear out (lose its communication appeal) very quickly. The accumulation of screens may drive frequency of exposure and commercial fatigue to new heights.

But there is also a significant upside to this phenomenon. If we no longer have to place the same message in two different screen media to accumulate reach, can we then create richer stories in each medium? We now have the opportunity to share the story across screens so that messages are additive as opposed to duplicative. This should liberate marketers and their agencies to craft rich brand stories as opposed to "one size fits all" video messages.

2. Distractions are now engagement. Not too long ago, the idea of media multi-tasking was a bad thing. We assumed that the act of engaging with multiple media at once diffused our attention and limited our ability to process content experiences. In the recent war of media budgets, various campaigns have sprung up by certain vested media interests to try to link single-minded focus with engagement. And, surprisingly, we all fell for it.

But, media convergence is actually creating a whole new phenomenon. Concurrent multiple media behavior may be the ultimate sign of engagement. What was once "multi-tasking" is now "multi-plexing." What if someone is so involved in a content experience that they will grab multiple devices to enhance their experience? Thanks to media convergence, this is now possible. And a few media brands and marketers are already starting to leverage the opportunity.

The Pioneers

Who were the pioneers of the media convergence movement? First and foremost, we have to give Apple the credit it is due. This brand, singlehandedly, understood the power and attraction of a brilliantly designed digital screen and gave us product innovation that changed the face of every device imaginable. Apple gave us content portability. Most content can be shared and/or experienced across Apple platforms. Now we can play our music on multiple devices and enjoy video experiences on any screen interface.

And, along with Apple's screen suite came a new form of digital content: the app. The app is truly a marvel. While the app may have started as more of a mobile media phenomenon, these self-contained content experiences can be downloaded onto any Apple screen device: iPhone, iPod, iPad, wherever! The app opened our eyes to the possibility that content can become platform neutral. Not surprisingly, the app has become big business. And other operating systems such as the Android are following suit.

While Apple was busy synchronizing digital screens, other bold content producers were toying with the possibilities offered by media convergence. They were creating transmedia stories. The early pioneers didn't have the benefit of video screen convergence. Henry Jenkins, in his book "Convergence Culture," tells the important story of "The Matrix." Through the use of film, comic books and video games (still relatively separate and distinct platforms), fans of "The Matrix" could deepen their experiences with the story line and the franchise in general. We learned a valuable lesson: Fans are willing and eager to engage with compelling content in as many platforms as are available to them so long as the content is additive, as opposed to duplicative.

Television content producers took this idea and leveraged the video screen to deepen what was otherwise a "broadcast" experience. Back in 2007, HBO created the "Voyeur" project in support of its on-demand movie "The Watcher." This bold experiment turned the outside of an apartment building in New York City into a screen to portray various vignettes to the voyeur on the city streets. The experience was enhanced online through webisodes that provided rich back stories on each character vignette that appeared on the building. Ultimately, the on-demand movie "The Watcher" told the tale of what happens when a voyeur witnesses a murder through an apartment window. The experience was truly exponential in terms of the audience it reached and engaged. HBO understood that screen convergence wasn't a threat to a cable network; rather, each screen enhanced the overall experience and created a deeper level of engagement for the broadcast experience.

While HBO is known for pushing the envelope to create and tell powerful stories, it is not alone in the transmedia content movement. Broadcast networks also understand the power of leveraging multiple screens to create immersive content experiences for their fans. Each of the major networks has pioneering success stories: ABC's "Lost" (2004-2010), CBS's "Survivor" (2000-present), Fox's "American Idol" (2002-present) and NBC's "Heroes" (2006-2010) are all prime examples of the transmedia storytelling format.

Television producers are continuing to explore storytelling across multiple screens. Last summer, Bravo caught up to the multi-screen consumption of its audience. As a network spokesperson was quoted in Businessweek, "Our users tend to adapt before us. We're just tapping into it." In June 2010, viewers of the "Real Housewives" franchise on Bravo were treated to a multi-screen extravaganza. Loyal fans of the "Real

Housewives of New York City" could experience the finale across every screen medium imaginable: smart phones, tablets, computers and televisions.

The future of immersive, multi-screen content is here, NOW!

Chaos

How well do marketers understand and leverage the potential of media convergence? The industry is built around fragmented media silos that are left over from an era when the media were truly different. Until we break down the silos and acknowledge that the entire media world is now digital, we're in for big trouble. Who creates the transmedia video experience that can live across multiple screens? The mainline creative agency? The digital agency? The mobile agency? This is a big problem. Not only is the "who" in question, but we now have to fundamentally question the "what" that we place on those screens. And the solution may no longer be the 30-second television commercial that is simply played across every screen imaginable. Remember, thanks to media convergence, the laws of reach and frequency are no longer clear. If we simply place the same video content across multiple screens, we'll burn out!

The silos create problems not only for marketers, but also for the media who still wish to keep media platforms separate and distinct. In an Ad Age article published on November 22, 2010, we learned of several media companies seeking a new executive position of "Chief Digital Officer." The old media guard's attempt to keep "digital" in its place shows a lack of understanding of what media convergence truly means. You can't separate digital from the total media experience anymore. This thinking exposes the outdated mentality of some of the old-line media leadership. Media leaders can no longer have an analog orientation or a digital orientation. They must have a convergence orientation that is truly platform agnostic.

We started the chapter with a discussion of buzzwords. When big ideas are reduced to empty buzzwords, we're left with chaos. For several years now, the industry has bantered about the idea of being "platform agnostic." This is a big idea that's borne from a true understanding of media convergence. The problem, though, is that we currently pay lip service to the idea of being truly platform agnostic. The term is a smoke screen that hides the truth behind the smoke and mirrors. We're still a business that is stuck in silos.

Truth

There is a wealth of potential resulting from media convergence. The media can create immersive, multi-platform/multi-screen content experiences to enhance audience involvement with compelling content. Marketers no longer have to repeat the same message in every platform imaginable to accumulate reach. And we can begin to tear down the silos that have plagued the industry and impeded our ability to take the idea of "platform agnostic" from an empty buzzword to a practical reality. This is all easier said than done. So let's break this idea down into more bite-sized actions:

1. First and foremost, the media have to embrace their own convergence. It's time to push out the CEOs who think that hiring a CDO is a good idea. Perhaps the CDO should take the top job! Content producers should expand upon the pioneering practices of delivering immersive multi-screen experiences that can engage audiences on multiple levels. We need more HBO

Voyeur projects, and we should support those media producers who are willing to experiment with transmedia storytelling.

2. Next, we need to continuously refresh our reach and frequency models to ensure that the most up-to-date multi-screen behavior is represented in how we project the reach and frequency of our media plans. This requires a holistic, single-source view of media consumption across multiple screen devices ... even beyond Nielsen's three screens.

3. Then marketers will need to abandon the current practice of hiring separate agencies to craft specific messages in supposedly separate channels. On the flip side, marketers will have to resist the temptation to simply place their television commercial in every medium that accepts video content.

4. Finally, marketing campaigns have the potential to become transmedia expressions of the brand story. The marketing paradigm is actually no different from the content paradigm. If we put out great brand stories, consumers will choose to engage with them across multiple platforms.

Thanks to media convergence, this is all possible!

CHAPTER FIVE

GLOBAL TRUTH #2 SYMBIOSIS

Symbiosis (n): the living together in more or less intimate association or close union of two dissimilar organisms, a cooperative relationship.

(Source: Merriam-webster.com)

We are a species of hunters and gatherers. It's how we're wired. We hunt prey that fall beneath us in the food chain, and we gather materials to help us thrive. Both actions are essential to our lives.

But, for some reason, we focus on the "hunter" part of the equation, and we tend to forget the "gatherer" side of things. When we look at the systems in our world, we quickly try to figure out the food chain. What sits on top? What is going to get killed off? We expect to see winners and losers.

We rarely talk about the cornucopia of "stuff" that we collect to help us survive and thrive. Perhaps there's more drama in focusing on the kill, and it's less interesting on the surface to talk about the strange relationships that spring up among all the things we gather in our lives.

Such is the story with modern media consumption. We tend to gather an entire market basket of media to help us survive and thrive in our daily lives. Something new comes along, and we gather it up. We simply make more room in our repertoire. It's rare that we let go of anything. What are we left with? More hours of media consumption than the total number of hours in an actual day! And the only way this phenomenon can happen is if the media work with, as opposed to against, each other.

The Technology Isn't the Story

While in the previous chapter we could point to digitization of all media as the catalyst for the first global truth, convergence, there really is no technology story that can explain the phenomenon of symbiosis. Rather, the phenomenon is driven by human behavior. When a new medium comes along, we simply make room for it, and we create a new role/relationship for the existing medium. Skeptical?

Let's go all the way back to Gutenberg's printing press. This transformative media invention forever changed the face of communication. But why, approximately 300 years after the invention of Gutenberg's printing press, did Paul Revere make his infamous midnight ride? Why did town criers still exist? While the printed page offered a critical value, it could not replace or displace the value of word of mouth.

Even today, one of the oldest forms of human communication—word of mouth—is still considered among the top most influential modes of media and message delivery. We use other media to fuel conversations that take place via word of mouth. Conversely, our word of mouth often becomes the fuel for mass media content. The symbiotic relationship between one medium and another was formed.

We Keep Waiting for Winners and Losers, and It Just Doesn't Happen

Let's fast-forward from Revolutionary War times to the 20th century. During the 20th century, the face of the media changed to a degree unlike anything we had ever experienced before. The media world exploded with an unprecedented magnitude of media choices. If you look at a 20th century timeline of media innovation, you will be struck by the growth in platforms without the demise of others. Think about it. Can you recall a single media industry that has systemically collapsed? True, while formats have changed and several media properties have come and gone, that's going to happen. But what we are talking about here is the foundational structure of the media. It just keeps growing! And the only way such growth can be sustained is through symbiosis.

Enter the dawn of the 21st century. Despite the history lessons of the 20th century, the doomsayers are filling headlines with the predictions that "old" media will be displaced by "new" media. Why, at the dawn of the 21st century, are we talking about the fall of old media? What is happening now that leads us to believe that centuries of media cohabitation will suddenly change? We can't place the blame on our legacy systems or the academic theories that sit on our bookshelves. The idea that media is an ecosystem of winners and losers doesn't hold water: It's our own baggage that we have to deal with.

If You Need Proof, Just Look at Television and YouTube

Think of YouTube and the other "tube"... aka television. YouTube was launched as an Internet forum for creative self-expression. Hence, the tag line "Broadcast Yourself." But what wound up happening? YouTube became an online destination for repurposed television content: memorable scenes from television shows, commercials we like/dislike and then a plethora of parodies from this content. If you stripped away the content that is some form of a television derivative, you would be left with a much smaller universe of content worth viewing on YouTube.

While some of the old-guard media (e.g., Viacom) treated YouTube as a threat, others quickly realized the incredible potential offered by this new medium. Think of YouTube as a phenomenal sampling mechanism for television content. Think of YouTube as a destination where fans of particular TV shows can engage and re-engage with their favorite clips and outtakes. YouTube helps to build both trial and loyal TV viewers—without the hefty expense of audience "tune-in" campaigns.

And what does television bring to YouTube? The "old media" fill an important content inventory need for YouTube. With all due respect, most of us simply aren't talented enough to fill near unlimited bandwidth with content that is truly special and worth viewing by others. While there are always Justin Biebers to be discovered, there is also an awful lot of bad user-generated stuff clogging the bandwidth of YouTube. We can, therefore, propose that YouTube and television exist in a symbiotic relationship.

Why was there such a difference between the perception that YouTube was a threat to television and the reality that YouTube and television actually thrive in a symbiotic relationship? It all goes back to our misguided hunter mentality. We expected one medium to land on top of the food chain, at the expense of the other. While our thinking was misguided, our gatherer behavior saved the day. Just as the town crier could still exist in harmony with the printing press, we found a way to add YouTube to our already rich market basket of media experiences. And television remains!

Symbiosis Changes the Rules

Symbiosis will fundamentally change the way we think about how the media work together to build effects. Our approach to media mix (selecting the various combinations of media in a media plan) must shift to acknowledge that media do not work in isolation; rather, they work in relationship to and with other media.

Historically, we analyzed each medium's ability to reach and/or engage consumers in isolation. We pitted one medium up against others in our budget allocation decisions. We then built combinations of media based upon the thinking that layering would expand the opportunity to see the message and/or influence consumers at contextually relevant points in the decision-making process.

Thanks to symbiosis, we have the opportunity to explore how combinations of media support and strengthen each other's ability to do their job. We need to build new media mix models that capture the "symbiosis effect" and measure the influence of one channel on another.

Forget the hierarchy of effects. There are no clear media winners and losers in the mix. It's time to evaluate combinations of media that support and reinforce the big picture.

The Pioneers

How are the media themselves dealing with symbiosis? Some better than others. And, for the news media, symbiosis is a matter of survival. Back in August 2008, Pew Research introduced us to a new form of news consumer: the integrator. These "integrators" comfortably get their news from a mix of both traditional and online news sources (sounds like the gatherer side of the human condition in action). A full 18 months prior to the Pew Research report, *Time* magazine understood this phenomenon and made a bold move to capitalize upon the symbiosis between the magazine and online news sources.

On January 5, 2007, Time magazine issued its first Friday publication—a seemingly provocative move from the newsweekly standard, Monday publication date. In a letter to his readership dated January 6, 2007, titled, "A Changing Time," Managing Editor Richard Stengel shared the rationale: "The new publication date reflects the way the Internet is affecting pretty much everything about the news business. Today, our print magazine and TIME.com are complementary halves of the Time brand." Stengel and his team understood that the weekend offers a time for reflection. The magazine could serve its readers best by shifting its publication day to Friday. Let the Internet own the harried workweek and let Time magazine own a weekend for reflection and agenda setting. The two media platforms could now better support and reinforce each other.

Obviously, Time was onto something. Time magazine circulates 3.3 million copies of its magazine every week, reaching more than 19 million adults in the U.S. (Source: GFK/MRI Fall 2010 Survey). In the meantime, Time magazine's newsweekly competitors didn't fare nearly as well. Newsweek magazine was sold to Sidney Harmon for one dollar, and US News & World Report announced that it will cease publication of its newsweekly magazine and focus solely on special issues and online news reporting.

While many marketers are scratching their heads trying to figure out how to fit all these media into the mix, consumers are taking matters into their own hands. Consider the Snickers Betty White phenomenon. What started as a 30-second commercial that aired during the Super Bowl launched a movement among fans that took Betty White and the Snickers brand across several media platforms and into pop culture. What should have been one commercial exposure on February 7, 2010, launched a perpetual engagement that lasted through Mother's Day 2010, and beyond.

It all began with a single airing of a Snickers 30-second commercial during the Super Bowl. The commercial drew rave reviews among the press and fans in the post-Super Bowl "ad-o-sphere." Shortly thereafter, Betty White fans started a conversation that quickly swelled to a movement across Facebook advocating for Betty White to host "Saturday Night Live." Both the mainstream press and the producers of "SNL" took notice. Betty White was announced as the host for the May 8, 2010, Mother's Day episode of "SNL." The live broadcast was a smash success, drawing the highest audiences in recent "SNL" history. And the May 8th broadcast provided a perfect contextual frame for the re-airing of the Snickers Betty White commercial.

Post broadcast, the enthusiasm ensued with a rush online to experience the Betty White "SNL" content. Ultimately, the Betty White "SNL" episode became one of the most viewed programs on Hulu.com. These online video exposures created yet another context frame for additional airings of the original Snickers Betty White commercial. And the story continues.

The Snickers Betty White phenomenon could only happen if the media operate in symbiotic relationships. Each media platform played a critical role in the movement and reinforced what unfolded in other media. If you took any medium out of the story, the whole movement would have collapsed!

Leave it to one of the largest and among the oldest advertisers around to show us how to blaze new trails by leveraging symbiotic media relationships. Procter & Gamble's Old Spice brand showed us just how tightly linked social networks and video-serving media truly are. In the "Responses" campaign, Procter & Gamble and its agency Wieden + Kennedy used fan-generated scenarios delivered via Twitter and Facebook as inspiration for more than 180 video executions of the wildly popular Old Spice Body Wash "The Man Your Man Could Smell Like" television commercial. These special vignettes populated an entire YouTube channel to delight consumers and deepen engagement with the Old Spice brand. The results fueled both brand conversations and sales to exponential heights.

This case—and everyone associated with it—deserves every bit of hype and attention it's getting. Why? Because it demonstrates what can happen when you throw away rule books and create an interactive, multi-media experience that emulates how your audience uses the media. Could anyone accurately "count" the potential exposures from this campaign in advance, and with any certainty? Absolutely not! But the consumer behavior was there, and P&G/Wieden acted. And let's not forget the great television commercial that sparked the entire movement.

In both the Old Spice and Snickers examples, the most traditional of advertising forms was the catalyst for these important, pioneering stories. Sorry to disappoint, but there was no battle of old vs. new media. There were no media winners and losers. Rather, both pioneering cases illustrate rich brand experiences that build off what occurred on one media channel to create and enhance an experience in another.

Chaos

Unfortunately, we rarely build truly integrated media plans to capitalize on symbiosis. We often consider the potential of each channel in isolation. We study media consumption tables and allocate resources based upon audience reach potential, and sometimes we throw in context for good measure. We build the media mix "one channel at a time." And we then model the effects the same way. Did the television investment pay out? What was the ROI of the search campaign? How many people clicked on the online display ad? Did the radio campaign generate a lift in sales relative to the control area that didn't receive radio? What was the issue-specific audience to my ad in magazine "x"? These are the questions we ask. These questions simply do not fit the stories described above.

We often talk about content the same way as the media: one channel at a time! We're all too familiar with the term "social media campaign." But what does that really mean? The stuff we put on Facebook, MySpace or Twitter? Or the sum total of the content we place across media to engage consumers in a conversation? Unfortunately, we tend to consider content for a specific channel and leave the big picture behind. Furthermore, our recent efforts to steer consumers to other pieces of content are pretty lame. Simply placing a website address or Facebook icon at the end of a TV spot is no more than paying lip service to a much bigger idea.

Even if we start off with an integrated approach, our efforts often tend to fall apart when the dreaded budget cut arrives. Even if our intention was right at the onset, we tend to unravel media plans based upon which medium is most flexible, or cancellable. We are often left with "half" conversations that aren't supported and/or reinforced in other media.

Too often, we look at the integration of our efforts at the end of the planning process. What does the media plan flowchart look like? Are all the channels in sync? We need to move this conversation forward. We need to start at the beginning as opposed to retro-fitting at the end!

Truth

In order to embrace symbiosis, we first have to study it. As more single-source data options become available to researchers, we will begin to understand inter-media effects in a whole new way. In the meantime, we can easily perform ethnographies to watch symbiosis in action with real consumers. Stop and think about your own media behavior. Chances are you can easily describe how parts of your market basket of media interplay and support each other.

Next, we need to change the way we approach the media mix. We should no longer build plans one channel at a time. Rather, we should build cross-platform conversations. This requires stopping and thinking about what you're going to say and then scheduling the combination of media that will support that particular conversation. For example, Old Spice understood that TV/YouTube/Twitter had to go together in order for its idea to work. If you take one channel out of the mix, the whole conversation falls apart.

In order to fuel a conversation, we need a new form of content. Content should draw you in and then across the media. This is how transmedia storytelling works. You start a conversation in one medium, and you deepen it across media that work in a symbiotic relationship with each other.

CHAPTER SIX

GLOBAL TRUTH #3
CIRCUITS

Circuit (n): the route traveled, a two-way communication path between points, the complete path of an electric current, including usually the source of electric energy.

(Source: Merriam-webster.com)

What do circuits and the basic principles of electric currents have to do with the media? Circuitry is a simple and powerful metaphor to describe how content flows across media channels from sender, to receiver, and back again. Once upon a time the media circuits (i.e., the pathways by which content flowed from sender to receiver) worked pretty much like a closed circuit. Content flowed from Point A to Point B with limited disruption. And each medium operated on its own circuit. Television content flowed across television circuits. Magazine content traveled along magazine circuits, and so on. The various media circuits ran parallel to each other. There wasn't much co-mingling.

Who flipped the switch? Content distribution and flow used to be in the hands of the "professionals": programmers, producers and marketers. And, most important, the consumer was the end point of all our efforts. They were the Point B, the recipients of what we called "push" marketing that traveled down closed media circuits.

When the media circuits were closed, advertising content could travel only as fast as the media channels could accumulate their audiences. We placed messages in specific channels and we waited, for a week, four weeks or for entire purchase cycles, to accumulate effects. The process was slow, cumbersome and expensive. We had to pay for every opportunity to see the communication. To make matters worse, media audiences would reach a plateau and our efforts would begin to pile up frequency and lead to message wear-out.

Content Doesn't Stay Put Anymore!

Someone and/or something opened the circuits! Content doesn't stay put anymore. It can start on one channel and seamlessly jump onto another. Some call it leaky media. Others call it displacement. Really, what we're talking about is this: Someone opened up the media circuits! How prolific is channel leaping? Just ask three famous women, and they'll tell you: The Mona Lisa, Susan Boyle and Tina Fey have all experienced the profound effects of open circuits.

If someone asked you to name the media channel that delivers the Mona Lisa to the world, you would most likely answer, "The Louvre." But that answer is only partially true. If you went to the Louvre, you would see hundreds of patrons standing before the Mona Lisa with their camera phones held high. With a simple click, and within only minutes, the Mona Lisa will travel across media circuits and her face will land on social network sites such as Flickr, Facebook and MySpace.

How did the world fall in love with Susan Boyle? She delivered an incredible performance on the British television stage that quickly leaped onto YouTube. But Susan's presence didn't stay fixed on YouTube for very long. Her performance traveled as a "must-see" link across e-mail servers and into our inboxes. We then followed her back to YouTube until the frenzy caught the attention of the American mass media. Once again, Susan Boyle became a broadcast phenomenon. But this time she was broadcast on another continent! The world had truly fallen in love with her story. And the cycle continues.

Tina Fey's "Saturday Night Live" renditions of Sarah Palin were a smash hit during the 2008 presidential election campaign. But, if you ask a classroom full of college students where they saw the vignettes, they will most likely tell you that they saw them on YouTube as opposed to on the "SNL" broadcast. Once again, the circuits were open and the content was displaced from its originating channel and onto an alternate platform.

The Technology That Opened the Circuits

What caused the circuits to open up? An empowered consumer armed with a few gadgets: a digital photo and/or video device (phone, camera, computer eye…take your pick), a scanner (sometimes) and a mouse. That's it! So long as content can be digitized, it can travel on/off/across nearly every media platform imaginable. Remember, thanks to media convergence, most media have some form of a digital structure. This makes it easy to open the circuits and move content around at the consumers' whim.

The act of movement becomes even more profound when you think about the incredible speeds by which this "channel leaping" occurs. Content can now flow as fast as a network connection—and that's fast! Think broadband, 3G and even 4G. This acceleration of content displacement across open circuits makes old media planning time feel like slow motion. Think about it. We used to count media plan intervals in weekly and four-week purchase cycles. Now we measure content distribution and flow based upon the speed of our connections. It's near instant!

Finally, all this displaced content needs someplace to go. Consumers can pull content off channels, but they can't easily put content back onto traditional media channels. That responsibility still lies in the hands of programmers, producers and marketers. Enter the social media networks (Twitter, Facebook, MySpace, YouTube etc.). We now have a place to post "stuff" that interests us. And, based upon the size of our networks, we can build a whole new audience for content.

The Liberation of Consumers: from Recipient to Accelerant

While the technology was necessary to open the circuits, the technology is simply an accomplice in a much bigger phenomenon. We have now fundamentally shifted the role of the consumer in the marketing paradigm. Some may call this "push" vs. "pull." This idea doesn't go far enough! Consumers do more than pull content along; thanks to open circuits, they can now accelerate great content experiences.

What do we mean by the idea of acceleration? Think about it. Now an engaged consumer can act in near real time and influence hundreds of people in their social networks. Word of mouth is now exponential. The idea of target audience reach is forever changed. Once we reach consumers, they now hold the power to amplify the reach of our efforts based upon the size of their e-mail distribution lists and the number of friends they have on Facebook. And those secondary audiences can do the same thing. It goes on and on…exponentially!

Consumers are now the most potent channel we have. Frankly, they always were. But now? Armed with the right technology, consumers can accelerate great content to vast networks at what I will call "The Speed of Share."

The Pioneers

Embracing the circuits takes a willingness to let go and put your fate in the hands of your customer. The indie rock band, Oasis, understood its fan base so well that it was willing to hand over the launch of its album "Dig Out Your Soul" to the very audience that would make its music a hit. This pioneer case turned every paradigm known to the music industry upside down.

Oasis understood that its fate was no longer tied to the promise of airplay from the once powerful disc jockeys. Rather, the band was truly successful when its music landed on the streets. So Oasis had the brilliant idea to start at the end. The band handed four tracks from its upcoming album over to noted street musicians in New York City. The idea was: Why not have fans discover the music and share the experience with others? And share they did! The street music became a groundswell that was shared via mobile media and tracked with geo-tagging. Oasis then captured the entire experience as a documentary film that aired on the band's MySpace page. Ultimately, the mainstream media covered the experience as a story as opposed to the traditional coverage of an album review. As a result, Oasis' "Dig Out Your Soul" became the first top-ten album the band had in more than 10 years.

What makes this case so special? If you ask the members of Oasis, they'll point to the album's success. But, for students of the media, this case demonstrates what can happen when a single piece of compelling content is shared freely by fans.

Think about it. A live street performance fueled media experiences across several different media channels: live (event), mobile/geo-tagged media, social media and mainstream media. Historically, we would have expected to produce very specific pieces of content to travel from Point A to Point B on fixed channels. We would need the songs themselves, music videos, concert tours, ads in music magazines, press interviews and a digital campaign to feed the individual requirements of fixed media channels. Not anymore. Oasis demonstrated that the media circuits are wide open and that an engaged consumer will accelerate the experience across media networks when the content "turns them on."

Finally, let's give credit where credit is due! The music, both the original music and the interpretations by the street musicians, was damn good and worth sharing!

How can we quantify the Oasis experience? What was the target audience reach and frequency generated by the experience? How many impressions did we accumulate during the purchase cycle? What was the ROI of each medium in the mix? These are all the wrong questions that we tend to ask. Because we're still stuck with those old, Newtonian media measures!

Chaos

The Oasis case was a brilliant demonstration of social media in action. But which medium was the social medium? Therein lays one of the biggest problems plaguing us today. We confuse the terms "social media" and "social networks." Social media is not a tactic. It is not a line item on a marketing plan, a specific channel or form of content. Rather, it is an outcome, and no single channel has a lock on the social nature of content. Every single medium is only one click removed from the conduit (the network infrastructure) that enables consumers to take the content and share it. Most any medium can serve as the originating medium in a journey that can take a great piece of content across open circuits and into vast networks of hearts and minds.

So how do we create integrated social experiences that can traverse open media circuits? We really don't know with any degree of certainty. And if any so-called experts claim to know the answers, don't believe them.

The rules are, indeed, thrown into chaos by the new and open circuits. The old-school rules of media effects were built for a time when the media circuits were closed, and each medium ran parallel to the other. Those old rules simply don't fit the open circuitry of the media today. Everything seems off. Our measures of media time, media place and media performance are now relative at best.

> **Time:** The traditional measures of media planning time—purchase cycle, average four-week or even weekly intervals—seems like an eternity when compelling content can travel across networks in nearly real time.

> **Place:** Media channel optimization seems a bit narrow-minded when content jumps off its originating channel and travels anywhere and everywhere. Which channel deserves the credit? Does it really matter anymore?

Performance: Measuring the opportunity to see via traditional reach and frequency on the front end misrepresents the actual engagement that transpires when consumers share content across their networks. We can only measure the first level of reach potential. What happens when reach turns to engagement and engagement turns to action? What happens when word of mouth becomes word of network?

Is there anything left to throw into turmoil? The very content that we place on the media must be worth sharing. Why in the world would anyone lift an interruptive, mediocre message off of one channel and send it across open circuits? They won't! Instead, they will vaporize any bad content that gets in the way.

Truth

If content can land anywhere and everywhere, have we returned to the Wild West of media planning? How can a media planner possibly develop and a marketer possibly approve a proposed media plan in the midst of such fluid behavior? We shouldn't throw informed strategy out the window, but we should change the way we approach channel optimization. The models need to capture how content leaps effortlessly off one channel and onto another. Which channel gets the credit for consumer engagement: the originating channel or the "jump" channel? The answer should be "all of the above."

It's time to put the consumer into the proper perspective. Consumers are not target audiences. A target is something you aim at—and shoot things at. Consumers are now the most powerful asset that we have. If we can engage consumers with great content, they will do a lot of the work for us. The media plan will take on a whole new shape and meaning. Our ideas will travel across more channels with greater speed, efficiency and impact.

We need to understand that counting the opportunity to see at the front end of our efforts in no way truly reflects the actual reach of the plan. The true reach of our efforts will be exponential thanks to the scope of each engaged consumer's network. We're better off saving the counting for the end!

Finally, you can launch great content in practically any medium and, if it's truly worth sharing, it will travel at an incredible speed among well-established networks of hearts and minds. But remember, content won't land anywhere—let alone everywhere—if it isn't worth sharing in the first place. We need to refocus our efforts toward the creative product, itself. Spoken from a true media professional, "Content was, is, and will remain king!"

CHAPTER SEVEN

GLOBAL TRUTH #4 BRANDS

Brand (n): a class of goods identified by name as the product of a single firm or manufacturer.

(Source: Merriam-webster.com)

What do the media have in common with the idea of branding? Unfortunately, not much ... yet! The media have long operated under a functional model that is based upon two foundational variables:

Distribution: This is the definition of the term "medium" in the first place. It's the idea that a medium represents a unique distribution pathway that enables content to flow from its source to an audience.

Audience: The focus here is the medium's ability to aggregate an unduplicated audience that is highly desirable to marketers.

And, once upon a time and not too long ago, this functional model seemed to work. Historically, media distribution pathways were relatively fixed and a bit more proprietary. Newspaper circulation networks were required to disseminate news to a particular community/market. Network television affiliates were required to broadcast television signals across a coverage area (Designated Market Area). The technology was not particularly friendly to redundant systems.

And audiences selected their medium of choice and spent their time with said medium ... usually to the exclusion of others. Media consumption analyses used to illustrate the "sea-saw effect." If you were a heavy user of one medium, you tended to be a light to non-user of another.

There was no need for the media to become true brands. Branding comes into play when product function is no longer enough. Brands take what are otherwise redundant products or services and make them special. Brands live beyond function, to infuse promises that create emotional bonds between the brand and the consumer.

Well, the time has come. The old model is broken: Any medium that defines its strategy by virtue of either its mechanism for content distribution and/or its ability to aggregate an audience will likely fail. There is nothing proprietary or particularly compelling in distribution pathways or audiences. The media themselves are becoming a commodity.

Technology Makes Media Redundant

Thanks to first digital and now wireless (mobile) technologies, new distribution platforms can and will spring up with limited cost or infrastructure required. Much like the human body that can generate a new blood flow when an arterial route becomes clogged, new media will find new distribution pathways to avoid any "clogs" in a metaphorical sense. Distribution pathways are no longer proprietary.

Think about it. Not too long ago, you needed a television set and a microwave relay signal to enjoy a television program. Now? That same program can be distributed over the air, via cable or satellite (live, DVR or on demand), on Hulu or perhaps through the .com version of the network. You could also possibly download the program through iTunes or order up a DVD or video stream from Netflix.

What about newspapers and magazines? You can still get them "on paper" delivered to your door. Or you can still find a newsstand and buy a single copy. But you can also read the e-version on your computer screen. Perhaps you will download an app that lives on your Kindle or your iPad. You can even get versions of this content served to your mobile phone!

What happened to the distribution pathways for music? We used to be limited by the bandwidth of the AM and FM spectrum. Not anymore. Now music travels via satellite and digitally. We can listen on radios, computers, televisions, MP3 players and our mobile phones.

The distribution pathway doesn't matter much anymore. The consumer has multiple choices. And chances are, in short order, another distribution pathway will spring up between the time this book goes to print (or possibly the e-version) and the time you read it!

If technology has rendered any single medium unnecessary, what's left for the media to do? The media must now take a lesson from every other category that deals with redundant products and services. The media must become brands!

The Pioneers

The commoditization of media will open up an opportunity for those who understand classic brand management and can apply these timeless principles to the media business. Media brands must live by the same rules as any other brand.

Call it what you like: brand essence, brand promise etc. The media must have a soul—a purpose/promise that defines its relationship between the content it delivers and the experience the audience expects. And this promise should be able to carry the brand beyond the boundaries of any particular media channel. The future rests with transmedia brands.

One media brand comes to mind as a true pioneer: someone who took what was otherwise a media commodity and made it special. Someone who, at the time, offered a provocative distribution platform. But this brand didn't rest on its laurels. It understood that its distribution platform wasn't the story. Its experience and promise to its audience would, ultimately, carry it forward across decades and numerous media platforms. That brand is: ESPN!

When ESPN first signed on the air back in 1979, the idea of a cable network that was fully dedicated to sports was quite provocative. But ESPN understood that cable distribution was not the big story. At the time, sports was fairly accessible. In any market, you could access sports across most any distribution platform: television, radio, newspaper etc. ESPN built a brand on the idea that it would not serve sports; it would serve the sports fan. The ESPN Mission reads as follows, "To serve sports fans wherever sports are watched, listened to, discussed, debated, read about or played." This notion of service to the fan shapes everything that ESPN does. It infuses a unique personality into the content offering and enables ESPN to expand wherever sports fans wish to engage with their passion. Cable network? Yes. Multiple cable networks, in fact! Radio network? Sure! Restaurant? Why not? So long as ESPN delivers a unique promise to the sports fan, the brand can travel well beyond the boundaries of any particular channel.

And, this Mission serves the ESPN brand well. In late September 2007, Forbes released a valuation of the top sports brands. ESPN took the top spot among sports businesses with a brand value of $7.5 billion!

Chaos

Unfortunately, we can count the number of true, transmedia brands in existence today on one hand (OK, maybe both hands). That's a big problem! Most media identities are still stuck in either their method of distribution or the audience they serve.

CNN: An acronym that forces the brand to be defined by a "cable." The CNN brand was originally built around a unique and provocative distribution platform for news. Clearly, this distribution platform is no longer unique or particularly compelling. News is consumed voraciously across every media platform imaginable. CNN knows this and has expanded its footprint across distribution platforms. But does CNN's cable audience automatically translate across distribution channels? Does the brand hold meaning beyond its acronym? CNN claims to be the "most trusted name in news." The notion of trust is an outcome; it's earned. What ultimately sits at the core of the CNN brand to earn the trust of the audience? The promise is unclear and the health of the CNN franchise reflects this ambiguity.

MTV: The music television brand that no longer plays music on television! MTV launched back in August 1981 truly as "music television"—a revolutionary idea that music could live on the television screen. The network helped to launch a whole new art form: the music video. That was then. This is now. The second MTV generation is no longer interested in a music experience on their televisions; rather, the favored method of music distribution is now a digital pathway. What's left for MTV? Jersey Shore!

What about More (the magazine for women of style and substance")? I like to call myself a "woman of style and substance," and I happen to enjoy More. But what does More magazine's positioning statement promise me? It tells me I'm in the right place: But why? Media brands must go further. Identifying the "who" is only half the brand equation. We need to know the promise that More will offer these women to forge meaningful bonds.

This problem isn't reserved simply for the old guard media. New/emerging media will realize the same fate if they cannot quickly adapt from technology darling to true brand. Whether you're a legacy medium or the newest innovation known to man, it's simple! We need more Real Simples! Enough said! The name speaks for itself. This brand promise is clear, relatable and applicable across platforms and audiences. The future is bright for transmedia brands.

But our problems are not limited to the state of the media themselves. Our troubles are compounded by the way marketers set marketing budgets. Marketers tend to allocate resources by channel—the very thing that we are rendering redundant and unstable! Marketing budgets by medium are not suited to take advantage of transmedia brand experiences. Let's revisit ESPN. In order to execute what we now call a "cross-platform" presence on ESPN, we have to tap into television budgets, digital budgets, radio budgets, magazine budgets, mobile budgets and possibly event budgets. It's an accounting nightmare!

And with those budgets, what are we shopping for? Media buyers and media sellers still fixate on audiences. Today, in a world of hyper media consumption, it is quite rare that any particular medium can and will attract a truly unduplicated audience that cannot be found elsewhere. Ask any media buyer, and they'll agree that no single media property is a "must buy" anymore. A buyer can literally "buy around" any property and still accumulate audience reach.

Truth

In a world where new technologies can spring up overnight, and no medium can claim ownership of its audience, your only hope is a powerful media brand that can move where the marketplace will go, and do so while remaining true to its promise. This should be the top priority for any "medium" in existence, today—old or new! In fact, it's a mandate for survival in media chaos.

But the opportunity doesn't stop with what we think of as media today. Marketers are quickly realizing the potential in converting their brands into transmedia brands as well. This notion of "brand as media" offers a whole new universe of possibilities in marketing. Stop and think about the power in the idea of Nike Plus. Is Nike Plus a product innovation or a community experience for passionate runners? Yes and yes! LEGO circulates one of the largest kids' magazines in the U.S., and it now has its own channel on Comcast on-demand. And Lexus publishes its own magazine that speaks to the tastes and interests of its drivers—just to name a few!

What does the idea of "brand as media" mean for the media? The very marketers who used to spend money with the media to advertise in their magazine, on their air etc. can now attract audiences with their own branded content! These marketers are becoming less reliant on traditional advertising in traditional media outlets in order to engage with their customers. Nike is now a formidable competitor to Runner's World for the running enthusiast's share of media time. Lexus now competes with Conde Nast Traveler! And kraftrecipes.com can give any epicurean media website a run for its money! Consumers will opt in to quality content experiences. If marketers can provide the experience better than the traditional media, so be it!

Frankly, marketers who understand branding may have an easier time morphing brands into media than those in the media business who don't have a clue about branding! Remember, the distribution pathway—the medium itself—is the easy part. It's the content that attracts audiences in this new world. When you think about "brand promises" and "brand attributes" as editorial guidelines for an engaging content experience, it starts to make a lot of sense.

And brand managers already understand the critical role of the consumer in the process. Customer experience, customer feedback and customer relationship management are already built into the brand management paradigm. Given that consumers now control the circuits (the Global Truth set forth in the previous chapter), the customer/brand interrelationship is a natural for "brand as media" initiatives. It's no wonder that the media experiences put out by traditional brands are more often co-created experiences with the consumer. Marketers understand this. The media are still catching up.

Transmedia brands will call for "transmedia accounting practices." Budgetary line items that force big ideas into media silos must give way to more holistic accounting. This is a problem on all sides. The media need to do a better job of selling one thing. Media buyers need to do a better job of evaluating one thing. Marketers need to do a better job of funding one thing. And that "one thing" is a holistic, transmedia content experience that engages consumers with brands. That one thing is the transmedia brand!

CHAPTER EIGHT

GLOBAL TRUTH #5
ECONOMICS

Economics (n): a social science concerned chiefly with description and analysis of the production, distribution and consumption of goods and services.

(Source: Merriam-webster.com)

In the end... it all comes down to money! The media business is a for profit enterprise. Nothing is sustainable that is given away for free. But, in media chaos, we're not quite so sure what part of the media model should make the money and what part should, ultimately, be free.

And, at the same time, marketers mandate (and deserve) value from their media investments. But what should they be valuing: the delivery mechanism, the audience and/or the experience?

So where is all the value in the media chaos economy? When Groupon turns down a $6 billion offer from Google, and Newsweek is sold to its new owner for one dollar, the whole idea of media valuation becomes interesting.

Do the fundamental economic laws of supply and demand make sense anymore? That's the key question we will set out to address in this chapter.

Technology Flipped the Supply-and-Demand Curve

Before the dawn of the digital media era, the media used to be in relatively limited supply. It was extremely costly and often times technically prohibitive to support an abundance of platforms. Broadcast media were limited by the bandwidth of the spectrum. And print media were limited by the costs of production (paper/ink/postage) and the costs of distribution (subscriptions and newsstands).

In this paradigm, it made sense that valuation was focused on the media. The media were in limited supply. Audiences didn't have much choice in the matter. They opted in to what was ultimately available to them. And the media accommodated these mass audiences by programming high quality content that had a mass audience appeal. In essence, we were operating in what we called a mass media economy.

Back then, there was only so much room for content. The media had to be much more selective. As a result, there was a lot of high quality content that didn't make it on the air or in print. The supply of content exceeded the media's capacity to place it all.

Once media became digitized, the supply equation forever changed. Thanks to digital effects, media capacity is no longer an issue. Price of entry is no longer daunting. Capacity is nearly unlimited and far exceeds our ability to fill all the bandwidth. Now? Media supply far exceeds actual demand.

What happens to the content supply equation when media capacity expands exponentially? All of a sudden, what used to be in excess is now scarce! There's a lot more room for a lot more content. And, while anyone can now become a "content creator," not everyone can produce high quality content that can attract an audience with much scale. High quality content is now the attractor. And the demand for high quality content now exceeds the supply of it.

Thanks to the digital effect, media are no longer scarce. Media supply is abundant. Valuation for the pipeline itself should decline (in theory). Now the economic attention should turn to content. If you follow the laws of supply and demand, high quality content experiences will drive value in the economics of media chaos.

The Pioneers

We have seen signs that content is more closely linked to price/value than connection (conduit) for quite some time. This trend is evident in nearly every sector of the media industry: television, music, newspapers and even books! The following pioneers are illustrating that their content is worth paying for, despite the state of the connection.

HBO is a true pioneer. We certainly don't need to pay for access to another cable channel on top of our already too-high cable bill. But millions of subscribers have placed HBO in a league of its own. Why? Because HBO produces dramatic television series unlike none other (think "The Sopranos," "Six Feet Under," "True Blood" etc.). And consumers are willing to pay a premium to engage with the HBO brand of preeminent storytelling. Despite the fact that consumers hate their cable companies and their high cable bills (more on that in a bit), more than 35 million subscribers add HBO to their cable suite, worth $3 billion in subscriber revenue, plus another $700 million in pay-per-view business (Source: Adweek Cable Hot List May 2010).

Back in 2007, the British band Radiohead allowed consumers to set the pricing curve for its new album, "In Rainbows." The album was openly accessible on the band's website. Radiohead acknowledged that consumers no longer want to pay for the distribution of music. So the distribution was, in essence, free. The real question: What was the content experience worth? It was up to each individual fan to determine what price to pay for the download. Not surprisingly, 60 percent of downloads went free of charge. But the other 40 percent commanded an average price of $8.05 per download (Source: Comscore). The fans set the demand curve, and the content experience paid it off. The album, "In Rainbows," received rave critical reviews. The music was great and worth paying for! In the end, fans bought 1.75 million "In Rainbows" CDs (Source: Wired October 16, 2008).

Further, when Kindle first launched we all fell in love with the platform itself. The idea of a digital book reader—now known more generally as an "e-reader" or a "tablet" was truly something special. But, in short order, the platform ran into "me-too" competition, and the price of the Kindle device dramatically declined. Along the way, the idea of Kindle as a platform gave way to Kindle as an e-reading experience. It didn't take long before we went from paying for the Kindle (hardware) to buying a Kindle app. The premise has shifted from medium to content. We now purchase access to all the Kindle content that can run on any hardware platform, Kindle or other!

And soon we will learn the true value of high quality newspaper content as The New York Times unveils its metered "Paywall" and the rest of the industry waits with bated breath. It's obvious that many consumers no longer see the value of paying for a paper medium to show up on their doorstep. The news is readily available online for free. But even the idea that The New York Times can begin to charge for usage suggests that, if consumers hold value to a particular brand of content, they will pay for it—even if the content in a more generic form is available to them for free. Why? Because The New York Times is a true media brand that transcends the notion of a local paper that delivers news to your doorstep. Ask anyone outside the New York Metro area why they read The New York Times, and they will share with you that the content experience is intelligent, thought-provoking and worthy of conversation. While the medium may no longer hold much value, the brand of journalism is still highly valued in the new media chaos economy.

Chaos

While there is mounting evidence that content is the real value driver, the media economy is stuck in a paradigm that assumes the media still have the ability to attract mass audiences. We still base financial transactions on the size of an audience to a particular medium during a specific time and place/space. Due to the vast explosion of media choices available today, the media no longer do such a great job of attracting mass audiences. The audience is now highly fragmented across many media and multiple content choices within each medium. As the audience to any single media opportunity declines in size, so does the media's ability to make money. And when the media make less money, they are then forced to reduce their investments in high quality content—the very thing that can still attract an audience! It becomes a downward spiral. As content quality declines, so will the audience. And so on.

When audience alone can no longer pay the bills, the media are then forced to turn to other revenue streams. The media start charging for access. Think about it: Consumers are now paying for "wires" or "wireless" access. The three screens—televisions, computers and mobile devices—will not work without some form of service provider. And, if you're like most consumers, you love to hate your provider. Why? Because there isn't much inherent value in the pipeline itself anymore. Most access is redundant. Supply is abundant, so who wants to pay that bill?

Let's put the two concepts together. What happens when the media charge access for an overabundance of low-quality content? The masses start to get angry! The Mission Statement of the website, tvalacarte.org, sums it up best: *"Our Pledge: I am fed up with my cable provider force-feeding me unwatchable programming, then raising my rates without notice. I am sick of complaining and I want action. I am hopeful that by joining this movement, together, we will combine our buying power to restore transparency and competition into the cable industry. No longer will Big Cable pick my programming, I will!"* (Source: tvalacarte.org)

This isn't just a television problem. The same holds true for most media. Let's take a look at satellite radio. The two service providers, Sirius and XM, were forced to merge and they still almost declared bankruptcy. Why? Because expanded bandwidth isn't worth much cost to consumers unless that bandwidth can be filled with valuable content. And, for Sirius/XM, it's an expensive proposition to pay for content that attracts audiences. Any guesses on the new contract terms that will keep the shock jock Howard Stern on Sirius/XM for another five years?

So, if channel capacity itself is devalued and content is the new attractor, how do the media respond? Unfortunately, many have opted to give their content away for free! Just take a look at the online versions of most local newspapers. For some strange reason, the media owners thought that consumers would continue to pay for access to a paper when the same content became available at their fingertips and on their computer screens for free. And we all know how that model is holding up. Many newspapers are in deep financial trouble.

Until we shift the pricing models to reflect the new supply-and-demand equation, media economics will remain in chaos.

Truth

Quality content (across any media platform) will drive economic prosperity in the new media economy. The pipeline will not hold its value as more options to connect keep emerging every day. But take the pipeline and transform it with something special, and the economic value will soar.

Just ask the team at Discovery Communications, and they will share how they are betting on the OWN (Oprah Winfrey Network) content experience on what was "Discovery Health" to significantly increase the valuation of the network. "We have a fantastic brand and, with Oprah behind us, we are looking to get more carriage for the channel and a different compensation structure over time," Discovery Communications CEO David Zaslav said. "Over time, distribution will grow and we will get meaningful fees for high quality content." According to SNL Kagan, Discovery Health attracts carriage fees of about 12 cents per subscriber per month. It has been estimated that OWN could attract rates as high as 40 cents to 50 cents per subscriber.

Given that legacy media systems already have the infrastructure in place to explore, invest in and ultimately promote high quality content, they will continue to have an important place in the media ecosystem. Let's not forget: High quality content is usually expensive. And it takes mass audiences to engage with said content to pay off such investments. For this very reason, mass media will continue to play an important role in a content-driven media economy. "Mass" makes money.

CHAPTER NINE

FIVE GLOBAL TRUTHS, ONE BIG PICTURE

During the course of this book, we identified and discussed in detail the Five Global Truths that can make sense out of a messy media world. They are summarized as follows:

1. Global Truth #1: Convergence

What used to be separate and distinct is now best described as the coming together of media platforms. Media are becoming strikingly similar, and it's all becoming a screen!

2. Global Truth #2: Symbiosis

We are not embroiled in a battle of old vs. new media. Rather, both old and new media tend to support and reinforce each other in symbiotic relationships.

3. Global Truth #3: Circuits

Media pathways, aka circuits, no longer run parallel to each other. Rather, the media circuits are now open and in the hands of an engaged consumer. Content can jump off one medium and onto another.

4. Global Truth #4: Brands

Media have outlived their functional utility. No single medium has a lock on distribution pathways and/or the audiences they serve. Media must adopt brand management practices in order to survive and to thrive.

5. Global Truth #5: Economics

Media is no longer in limited supply/high demand. We have more media than we know what to do with! Now the true value of the media rests with the content that fills the pipeline.

Five Global Truths, One Big Picture!

Are the Five Global Truths truly separate and distinct? Actually, they all start to come together, to create a stunning big picture. It all starts with the idea of *convergence*. The media are coming together as opposed to growing apart. This natural coming together of platforms creates a cooperation as opposed to a competition among platforms. When entities are similar and can benefit from each other, *symbiosis* forms. The collaboration among symbiotic systems makes it easier for content to travel off one platform and onto another. The *circuits* will inherently open up. No single medium can own the content or the audience in an open environment. The attractors become *brands* who consistently deliver high quality content experiences across platforms. And this all fundamentally reshapes *economics*. Value shifts from the audience to any given medium to transmedia content that can engage an audience across multiple media. The Five Global Truths illuminate one big picture of how the media world works today.

When you take a step back and think about this new media order, all of a sudden what was once chaotic seems to make a whole lot of sense! The media world doesn't look as complex. A new order that's governed by similarities and cooperation is much easier to deal with than the old world where every single medium had to be dealt with on its own and with its own set of rules.

This coming together of media systems should make it easier for us to remain focused on the big picture and to harness the exponential potential of the media channels in the new law of energy: C^3. Really, what we're dealing with now is a new relationship between content, consumers and channels.

C (1): Content

First and foremost, we must relentlessly focus on content worth sharing. Content is the ultimate attractor in an open media system. Mediocre content, whether its primary purpose is entertainment or marketing, simply won't cut it. We need to relentlessly focus on storytelling in ways that further engage consumers across a suite of symbiotic media platforms. We must develop transmedia brands that can deliver transmedia brand stories. This is an equal opportunity proposition: Both the media and the marketers who advertise on the media can play in this space. Those who understand content-driven brand experiences will win. The first to adapt to transmedia brand management with engaging storytelling will set the future for integrated marketing success.

C (2): Consumers

Next, we must place consumers at the center of our efforts so that they, in turn, can accelerate brand momentum. This is much larger than "consumer insight" or "customer centricity." We must acknowledge that consumers have always been and will continue to be the most potent media channel in any media plan. We must engage consumers beyond the point of purchase to a new point of acceleration. We should think of lifetime value not only in terms of brand loyalty, but also in terms of brand advocacy. To what lengths will an engaged consumer go to perpetuate the brand's marketing story?

C (3): Channels

Ultimately, we must fully embrace the exponential potential of a new media world that is guided by the Five Global Truths. It's time to let go of the old Newtonian media rules that simply don't make sense anymore. We cannot hunt audiences down at the expense of declaring some media as the winners and others as the losers. We have to understand how the media truly work together to create multi-layered and engaging consumer experiences.

Media allocations can no longer be an either/or exercise; they must now represent the combinations of symbiotic media occurrences that round out the consumer experience. The walls between digital media and the rest of the media world must come down. It's all becoming digital, and the sooner we all realize that every medium imaginable is now digital, the better! We must change what we value. A discrete audience measurement in any specific medium at any specific point in time is a very small measurement of the total potential of integrated marketing communication. If consumers accelerate brand experiences across vast networked media channels, the true measure of our efforts cannot possibly be known.

And, we have to get comfortable with that! We may have explained media chaos, but it will remain a bit messy!

CHAPTER TEN

PUTTING NEW THINKING TO WORK

How can C^3 unfold as a new media and message delivery process? For those of you who are new to the world of marketing and media, you're in great shape! You do not have to unlearn all the legacy methods that have plagued the rest of us for quite some time. And, for those of you who have been around for a while, go grab a clean sheet of paper! You'll need it!

Luckily, this new approach is much easier to implement than past media planning methods that relied upon complicated media mix models and an obsessive focus on calculating opportunities to see. Now we need a few simple tools and one big picture: We need a great story to tell (across multiple channels), we need an engaged consumer and we need an open media architecture that enables consumers to accelerate content across media channels and social networks. We still need to measure effects, but we can now shift the burden of measurement from optimizing opportunities to optimizing outcomes.

Start With a Good Story. Do Not Pass 'Go' Until You Have One!

For years, we have been embroiled in a heated debate. What comes first: the medium or the message? Actually, neither medium nor message matters in a narrow sense. Rather, the first step in the process is to develop a highly engaging transmedia story. A story is much larger than a "message." A transmedia story is a brand narrative that can involve consumers across time and media platforms. If we don't have the story, the rest of the process really doesn't matter.

Fund Combinations of Media Based Upon How They Work Together to Support the Story

Next, we need to allocate resources in a whole new way. We need to fund combinations of media that work together (in symbiosis) to support/reinforce key elements of the transmedia story. We can no longer fund each individual media channel in isolation; we must now fund media in combinations based upon how they truly work with each other. What was once separated in most marketing and media functions will now join together.

Think of the possibilities. Perhaps now social networks and broadcast media will be planned and funded as one effort. Or perhaps broadcast radio and mobile media will now be considered in tandem. Marketing organizations and their marketing services agencies will have to do more than coordinate efforts. They will have to truly plan and implement these efforts as one, integrated experience. Cross-platform media planning and buying will become the norm. There will be more marketplace incentives for the media themselves to evolve into transmedia brands that can offer marketers truly platform-neutral solutions.

Hand the Media Plan Over to Consumers

During the two previous phases of the process, the consumer is still a recipient of controlled content experiences (controlled by the media and/or by the marketers). Next, we have to let go and hand over control to consumers. In fact, we don't have to do much of anything! Considering that the media circuits are wide open and ready for consumers to "play" with content, we simply have to inspire consumers and engage them to the point of acceleration. Consumers will, by default, interact with content. They will either (a) vaporize bad content or (b) accelerate great content. Our hope is to convert consumers from message recipients to message accelerants. Think of this as a conversion phase whereby consumers become the most valuable media channel in the entire mix.

Once consumers are converted from recipients to accelerants, the media plan in the real world should no longer bear any resemblance to the media plan on paper. If all goes well, the controlled schedule of content across media channels will quickly go out the window! Thanks to open media circuits, content will travel on/off/across more media touch points and reach more consumers than we can possibly imagine or measure with any degree of certainty.

Support and Reinforce an Ongoing Conversation

At this juncture, what's left for a marketer to do? Sit back and watch/wait? Well, not exactly. A marketer's job is to continue to fuel momentum by ensuring that storytelling remains fresh, provocative, brand-relevant and accessible. At times, marketers may need to provide additional investment in specific media clusters to support/reinforce specific elements of the transmedia story. A marketer's job is to listen, reflect and then respond. A marketer must now enter into a collaborative partnership with consumers and use the media as a shared resource for shaping and delivering an ongoing conversation.

Measure What Truly Matters

Finally, we must measure the total outcome of our efforts. If the Five Global Truths teach us anything at all, they suggest that the media no longer work in isolation. The idea that we should measure the effects of a single media channel in an integrated media plan seems very small when you consider the true interdependence of the media. The traditional valuation of media audiences captures only one small slice of the total picture. We should care less about the opportunities to see a controlled marketing message and focus more on the collective experience and the final outcome of our efforts. We must shift our measures from the beginning of the process to the end.

And we have to accept the fact that it may be impossible to measure the total reach of our efforts if all goes well. We may now finally be liberated to measure what counts: return on objectives and outcomes (ROO) based upon customer sales and customer value.

Proof Delivered by the Pioneers Themselves

This new process was not engineered in a conference room; rather, it was the result of observing how the pioneers (and their stories) described and celebrated throughout the pages of this book got things done. In each instance, we can relate back to a powerful piece of content that lent itself to all the potential of transmedia storytelling. Each situation described unique combinations of media channels that worked together to engage and inspire consumers in the story. If the depth and breadth of media combinations described throughout the book is any indication of what the future holds, the possibility for collaboration among media channels appears endless!

We do not have to restructure ourselves around new media pathways; rather, we need to remain open and flexible to consider how all the media can work together to carry a story. Further, in every instance, the pioneering case relied heavily upon authentic and heavy engagement by consumers. In each case, the pioneer didn't buy its way into the relationship or force a "social" conversation. Rather, consumers opted to engage with and to share the experience based upon the quality and resonance of the story. And, when they truly engaged, the sky was the limit.

No one could possibly build a media plan flowchart to chart the course of Snickers' Betty White or Oasis "Dig Out Your Soul" until the journey was complete. But that didn't mean that the marketers remained idle. They contributed additional content in additional media to keep their stories vibrant and engaging. And, finally, it's doubtful that Old Spice worried much about the cost to add Twitter to the "Responses" campaign. Or if Bravo did an ROI analysis on one screen component of the "Real Housewives" finale experience. The pioneers were relentlessly focused on a much bigger picture. A valuable lesson learned indeed!

Now It's Your Turn!

It's time for me to head back into the classroom to inspire another generation of integrated marketers. Hopefully, this text has inspired you to think about the world of media in a whole new light! Now it's your turn to forge new pathways in a new media world. With the Five Global Truths as your compass, you can now explore an abundance of new possibilities. Perhaps, you will become the next pioneer that will continue to show us how it's done!

ACKNOWLEDGMENTS

I couldn't possibly attempt to write this book without the lasting impressions of so many people who have inspired me during the course of a 25-year career. I am truly grateful that I have enjoyed (and continue to enjoy) opportunities to collaborate with the best and brightest minds in marketing, advertising, media and academia.

There are too many people to thank individually. Behind each company mentioned here, there is a host of individuals who made my experiences truly special. My heartfelt thanks goes to Leo Burnett for its indelible stamp of "Human Kindness" on the business of advertising. Thank you to the former leaders of TLK for recognizing and celebrating young talent. They created a second family that knew no boundaries both in how we worked and our impact in the marketplace. Thank you to Starcom Worldwide for blazing new trails in the media world while remaining steadfastly committed to integrity and client service. I owe a debt of gratitude to Energy BBDO for embracing the idea that a creative media mind can make "The Work" better. And, finally, thank you to Medill, Northwestern University, for opening its doors to a practitioner with a passion for lifelong learning.

I also wish to acknowledge and express my gratitude to the many marketers who entrust their agency partners every day with their most valuable assets: their brands. Thank you to the Procter & Gamble Company for 10 years of strategic discipline that bests any MBA program around! Thank you to Allstate for being at the forefront of considering creative ideas beyond the storyboard and in the context of real media plans. Thank you to the William Wrigley Jr. Company for mandating that World Class Communication is borne from the integration of content and connection. And thanks to LEGO for its continued partnership and its relentless support of innovative ideas, even when the empirical proof doesn't yet exist.

Finally, this book didn't come together by itself. I received support and encouragement from many people along the way. First, I would like to thank Tom Collinger for giving me an opportunity to enter "Chapter Two" of my career and for challenging me to bring truly cutting-edge thinking into the classroom. I would like to thank Bruce Bendinger for suggesting an organizing structure for the presentation of the Five Global Truths. I would also like to thank Don Schultz and Mike Moynihan for their honest assessment of the manuscript in its draft stages. I would like to thank my editor, Mary Leader, for keeping this book short and to the point. And, finally, I wish to thank my husband, Steve, for supporting me in everything that I attempt to do.

CITATIONS

Chapter One

The foundation of Moore's Law can be found in his white paper: Moore, Gordon E. "Cramming More Components Onto Integrated Circuits." *Electronics* 38, no. 8 (1965): 114-17.

Chapter Two

Jenkins, Henry. "Transmedia Storytelling Definition." In *Convergence Culture,* 293. New York: New York University Press, 2006.

Maiville, Mark. "A 'Thin Sliced World': New Methods, Models and Systems for Media Audience Analysis." White paper presented at ARF: Audience Measurement 2.0 Conference, New York, NY, June 26-27, 2007.

Chapter Four

Gillette, Felix. "For Bravo, One Screen Isn't Enough." *Bloomberg Businessweek*, November 2010, 9-14.

Learmonth, Michael. "Old Media Decides Digital Still Needs a Chief." *Ad Age*, November 22, 2010.

Chapter Five

Pew Research Center. "Key News Audiences Now Blend Online and Traditional Sources: Audience Segments in a Changing

News Environment." Washington DC: Pew Research Center for the People & the Press, August 17, 2008.

Chapter Seven

Ozanian, Michael K., and Peter J. Schwartz. "The World's Top Sports Brands." Forbes.com, September 27, 2007.

Chapter Eight

"For Radiohead Fans, Does 'Free' + 'Download' = 'Freeload'?" comScore Press Release, November 5, 2007. Contact: Andrew Lipsman.

Crupi, Anthony. "Cable Hot List." *Mediaweek*, May 9, 2010.

Seidman, Robert. "Oprah's Move to Cable All About the Big Money of Higher Carriage Fees." tvbythenumbers.com, February 10, 2010. Discovery CEO quote within article sourced via Multi Channel News.

Van Buskirk, Eliot. "Radiohead's In Rainbows Outsold Previous Albums Despite Giveaway." Wired.com, October 16, 2008.

SUGGESTED READING

Block, Martin P., and Don E Schultz. *Media Generations. Media Allocations in a Consumer-Controlled Marketplace.* Worthington, OH: Prosper Business Development Corporation, 2009.

> ***Author's Pick:*** *The front-half of* Media Generations *clearly illustrates how the state of the media has evolved over time and by consumer target group. Read this book, and you will never believe in an Adult 18-49 demo again!*

Garfield, Bob. *The Chaos Scenario.* Nashville, TN: Stielstra Publishing, 2009.

> ***Author's Pick:*** *Bob Garfield has an uncanny wit and sense of humor to add levity to all the disruption in the media business. In 2009, Bob blew things up. In 2011, we will reconstruct the landscape with the Five Global Truths!*

Jenkins, Henry. *Convergence Culture: Where Old and New Media Collide.* New York, NY: New York University Press, 2006.

> ***Author's Pick:*** Convergence Culture *is a phenomenal introduction if you're new to the concept of transmedia storytelling.*

Schultz, Don, and Heidi Schultz. *IMC, The Next Generation: Five Steps for Delivering Value and Measuring Financial Returns.* Chicago, IL: McGraw-Hill, 2003.

> ***Author's Pick:*** *This is a must read for anyone working in marketing.* IMC, The Next Generation *wrote the rules of customer-centric marketing.*

FURTHER INSPIRATION

Old Spice Responses Case Study:
http://creativity-online.com/work/old-spice-responses-case-study/20896

Oasis Dig Out Your Soul Case Study:
http://creativity-online.com/work/oasis-streetwise-case-study/15508

HBO Voyeur Case Study:
http://www.youtube.com/watch?v=QCr853VVo9c&feature=channel_video_title

Hero Creator Tim Kring on Transmedia Storytelling:
http://www.youtube.com/watch?v=jWyo00IoXo8&feature=channel_video_title

To learn more about ESPN's Transmedia Strategy, visit their website:
http://www.espncms.com/index.aspx?id=166

Bob Garfield's NPR Podcast:
http://www.npr.org/templates/story/story.php?storyId=4583366

25420499R00059

Made in the USA
San Bernardino, CA
29 October 2015